ESHET CHAYIL - אשת חיל

Rediscovering the Courage, Wisdom & Strength Within

Elizabeth Shulam

TABLE OF CONTENTS

ESHET CHAYIL
אשת חיל -

Rediscovering the Courage, Wisdom &
Strength Within

Elizabeth Shulam

To the godly women in my family—
those who came before me,
those who walk beside me,
and those who will come after.
Your faith shaped my foundation.
Your strength steadied my steps.
Your prayers carried me farther than you ever knew.
This book is dedicated to your courage,
your wisdom,
your quiet sacrifices,
and your unwavering trust in God.
Your legacy is my inheritance.
Your example is my blessing.
Your valor is the story I carry forward.

I have been richly blessed.

Virginia Elizabeth Lawless Manning Mayes
Elizabeth Ellen Barneycastle Plott Whitten
Emma Elizabeth Manning Plott Hodnett
Maude Viola Cannaday Hollandsworth
Roberta June Cummins Saunders

Marcia Gail Saunders Shulam, of righteous memory. You
embodied eshet chayil. Happy Birthday.

and my mother:
Janice Rebecca Plott Hollandsworth.
The rock I was built upon.

CONTENTS

PREFACE

Elizabeth Shulam

Every woman carries strength within her—strength she may recognize easily, strength she may question, and strength she may not yet see at all. Over the years, I have met women in every season of life who quietly wondered if they were doing enough, becoming enough, or measuring up to the version of "godly womanhood" they had been shown. Many were drawn to the idea of the Proverbs 31 woman, yet felt weighed down by the way she is often presented: flawless, tireless, endlessly productive, and always composed.

But that is not the picture Scripture gives us.

The Hebrew phrase at the center of Proverbs 31—*Eshet Chayil* (אשת חיל)—does not mean "perfect woman." It speaks of valor. Of strength. Of courage shaped from the inside out. It is the same word used to describe warriors and leaders—people of substance, resilience, and quiet fortitude. This phrase was never meant to function as a checklist. It reads more like a celebration.

And more than that, it sounds like a blessing.

This book grew out of a desire to rediscover that blessing and to restore the heart behind it. Over time, I have watched women walk through seasons of enormous transition—young adulthood, motherhood, loss, leadership, waiting, disappointment, new beginnings, and the quiet years of spiritual maturity. And in each of those seasons, I have witnessed something steady and often unnoticed taking shape. Strength emerging quietly. Faith deepening without fanfare. Wisdom forming through lived experience. Kindness offered in ways that changed lives. Courage expressed not through certainty, but through trust when clarity had not yet arrived.

Those stories—both the ancient ones preserved in Scripture and the modern ones unfolding around us—have shaped these pages.

You will meet Ruth, Hannah, Deborah, and Sarah again here, though perhaps with new eyes. You may begin to notice how closely their seasons mirror our own, and how strength grows not in ideal conditions, but in the real, complicated terrain of ordinary life. Scripture consistently honors the woman whose heart is rooted in God, whose hands serve with intention, whose words bring life, and whose faith quietly shapes her future.

This is not a book about becoming someone else. It is about remembering who God has been shaping you to be all along.

As you read, I invite you to slow your pace and let these chapters meet you gently. There is room here to reflect, to rest, to wonder.

There is space to notice the strength that has been forming within you—sometimes quietly, sometimes boldly, often slowly, and always faithfully.

May these pages encourage you.
May they remind you of the courage you already carry.
May they bless the season you are in, just as it is.

And may they awaken a deeper awareness of the truth Scripture speaks over you:

You are *Eshet Chayil*.
A Woman of Valor.
Strong in every season.

INTRODUCTION

You have probably experienced this moment before. Proverbs 31 is mentioned—in a sermon, a study group, or a passing conversation—and something inside you tightens just a little. Some women feel inspired by it, but many feel overwhelmed. The chapter has often been treated like a résumé of ideal womanhood, a collection of accomplishments quietly inviting comparison rather than offering encouragement.

For others, Proverbs 31 has been reduced to a narrow stereotype—the perfect wife, the tireless homemaker, the endlessly cheerful servant. Yet the closer you look at the text itself, at its language and context, the more you realize that this woman is not being presented as an unreachable standard.

She is being honored for her strength.

The opening phrase sets the tone: *Eshet Chayil*—a Woman of Valor.

That word, *chayil* (חַיִל), carries weight. It is the same word used to describe warriors. It appears in the stories of Gideon and David, and among the mighty men of Israel. It speaks of courage and capability, of resilience and resolve. Nothing about it is ornamental. It belongs to someone who stands steady in the face of difficulty and knows who she is before God.

That understanding alone begins to shift how Proverbs 31 is heard.

This book lives in that shift. It is not a manual for becoming the "perfect woman"—that would miss the point entirely. It is an invitation to become a grounded one. A courageous one. A woman whose faith is steady rather than fragile, whose kindness carries truth, and whose wisdom shapes the rhythm of her days. Scripture rarely presents strength as loud or showy. More often, it appears quiet, consistent, and deeply faithful.

In many Jewish communities, Proverbs 31 is recited each week as a blessing—spoken or sung over mothers, daughters, sisters, wives, and single women alike. It is not used as a measuring stick, but as a way of saying, "You are valued. You are strong. You reflect the image of God in ways that matter." That posture—a blessing rather than a burden—beats at the heart of this book.

You will walk through the stories of four women who embody valor in different seasons: Ruth in young adulthood, Hannah in motherhood, Deborah in leadership and maturity, and Sarah in her later years. Strength is not one-size-fits-all. It takes different shapes across a lifetime, and God meets us uniquely in each season.

Along the way, you will also encounter gentle, practical ways of cultivating faith, wisdom, and kindness within the rhythms of everyday life. These are not offered as additional tasks to perform, but as ways of shaping the kind of inner strength Proverbs 31 celebrates.

Whether you come to these pages from a place of confidence or from a place of weariness, whether you are single or married, a mother or not, young or seasoned, this journey is for you. Strength is not reserved for a select few. It is the work God is continually doing in us as we learn to trust Him in every season.

My prayer is simple. That as you read, you will begin to see yourself as Scripture sees you—not as someone striving for perfection, but as someone called to walk with courage, depth, and purpose. As *Eshet Chayil*. A Woman of Valor.

This journey begins with identity. And once that truth settles in, everything else begins to take shape.

Let's begin!

ESHET CHAYIL

Here is the full poem in Hebrew, one verse per line:

אֵשֶׁת־חַיִל מִי יִמְצָא ,וְרָחֹק מִפְּנִינִים מִכְרָהּ.

בָּטַח בָּהּ לֵב בַּעְלָהּ ,וְשָׁלָל לֹא יֶחְסָר.

גְּמָלַתְהוּ טוֹב וְלֹא רָע ,כֹּל יְמֵי חַיֶּיהָ.

דָּרְשָׁה צֶמֶר וּפִשְׁתִּים ,וַתַּעַשׂ בְּחֵפֶץ כַּפֶּיהָ.

הָיְתָה כָּאֳנִיּוֹת סוֹחֵר ,מִמֶּרְחָק תָּבִיא לַחְמָהּ.

וַתָּקָם בְּעוֹד לַיְלָה ,וַתִּתֵּן טֶרֶף לְבֵיתָהּ ,וְחֹק לְנַעֲרֹתֶיהָ.

זָמְמָה שָׂדֶה וַתִּקָּחֵהוּ ,מִפְּרִי כַפֶּיהָ נָטְעָה כָּרֶם.

חָגְרָה בְעוֹז מָתְנֶיהָ ,וַתְּאַמֵּץ זְרוֹעֹתֶיהָ.

טָעֲמָה כִּי־טוֹב סַחְרָהּ ,לֹא יִכְבֶּה בַלַּיְלָה נֵרָהּ.

יָדֶיהָ שִׁלְּחָה בַכִּישׁוֹר ,וְכַפֶּיהָ תָּמְכוּ פָלֶךְ.

כַּפָּהּ פָּרְשָׂה לֶעָנִי ,וְיָדֶיהָ שִׁלְּחָה לָאֶבְיוֹן.

לֹא־תִירָא לְבֵיתָהּ מִשָּׁלֶג ,כִּי כָל־בֵּיתָהּ לָבֻשׁ שָׁנִים.

מַרְבַדִּים עָשְׂתָה לָּהּ ,שֵׁשׁ וְאַרְגָּמָן לְבוּשָׁהּ.

נוֹדָע בַּשְּׁעָרִים בַּעְלָהּ ,בְּשִׁבְתּוֹ עִם זִקְנֵי־אָרֶץ.

סָדִין עָשְׂתָה וַתִּמְכֹּר ,וַחֲגוֹר נָתְנָה לַכְּנַעֲנִי.

עֹז וְהָדָר לְבוּשָׁהּ ,וַתִּשְׂחַק לְיוֹם אַחֲרוֹן.

פִּיהָ פָּתְחָה בְחָכְמָה ,וְתוֹרַת חֶסֶד עַל לְשׁוֹנָהּ.

צוֹפִיָּה הֲלִיכוֹת בֵּיתָהּ ,וְלֶחֶם עַצְלוּת לֹא תֹאכֵל.

קָמוּ בָנֶיהָ וַיְאַשְּׁרוּהָ ,בַּעְלָהּ וַיְהַלְלָהּ.

רַבּוֹת בָּנוֹת עָשׂוּ חָיִל ,וְאַתְּ עָלִית עַל כֻּלָּנָה.

שֶׁקֶר הַחֵן ,וְהֶבֶל הַיֹּפִי ;אִשָּׁה יִרְאַת יְהוָה ,הִיא תִתְהַלָּל.

תְּנוּ־לָהּ מִפְּרִי יָדֶיהָ ,וִיהַלְלוּהָ בַשְּׁעָרִים מַעֲשֶׂיהָ.

Proverbs 31:10–31

Verse	Transliteration	English (paraphrased meaning)
31:10	*Eshet chayil mi yimtza, ve-rachok mipninim mikrah.*	A woman of strength and valor—who can find her? Her value is far beyond precious jewels.
31:11	*Batach bah lev ba'lah, ve-shalal lo yechsar.*	Her husband's heart trusts her; he lacks nothing of gain.
31:12	*Gemalathu tov ve-lo ra, kol yemei chayyeha.*	She brings him good and not harm, all the days of her life.
31:13	*Darshah tzemer u-fishtim, va-ta'as be-chefetz kappéha.*	She seeks out wool and flax, and works with willing, eager hands.
31:14	*Hayetah ka-oniyot socher, mi-merchak tavi lachmah.*	She is like merchant ships, bringing her food from far away.
31:15	*Va-takom be'od layla, va-titten teref le-veitah, ve-chok le-na'aroteha.*	She rises while it is still night, providing food for her household and tasks for her servant girls.
31:16	*Zamemah sadeh va-tikkachehu, mi-pri kappéha nat'ah kerem.*	She considers a field and acquires it; from what her hands have earned, she plants a vineyard.
31:17	*Chag'rah ve-'oz motneha, va-te'ammetz zeroteha.*	She girds her loins with strength and makes her arms strong.
31:18	*Ta'amah ki tov sachrah, lo yikhbeh ba-layla nerah.*	She senses that her trading is good; her lamp does not go out at night.

31:19 *Yadeha shil'cha va-kishor, ve-kappéha tam'chu pelech.* Her hands stretch to the distaff, and her fingers grasp the spindle.

31:20 *Kappah parsah le'ani, ve-yadeha shil'cha la-evyon.* She opens her palm to the poor and extends her hands to the needy.

31:21 *Lo tira le-veitah mi-sheleg, ki chol veitah lavush shanim.* She does not fear for her household when it snows, because they are all clothed in warm garments.

31:22 *Marbaddim as'tah lah, shesh ve-argaman levushah.* She makes coverings for herself; her clothing is fine linen and purple.

31:23 *Noda ba-she'arim ba'lah, be-shivto 'im ziknei-aretz.* Her husband is known at the city gates, where he sits among the elders of the land.

31:24 *Sadin as'tah va-timkor, va-chagor natnah la-k'na'ani.* She makes linen garments and sells them; she supplies belts to merchants.

31:25 *'Oz ve-hadar levushah, va-tischak le-yom acharon.* Strength and dignity are her clothing, and she can look to the days ahead with joy.

31:26 *Piha pat'cha be-chokhmah, ve-torat chesed al leshonah.* She opens her mouth with wisdom, and teaching of kindness is on her tongue.

31:27 *Tzofiyah halichot veitah, ve-lechem 'atzlut lo tochel.* She watches carefully over the ways of her household and does not eat the bread of idleness.

Kamu baneha va- 31:28 *ye'ashruha, ba'lah va-yehallel'ah.*

Her children rise up and call her blessed; her husband also, and he praises her.

31:29 *Rabot banot 'asu chayil, ve-at 'alit 'al kullanah.*

"Many women have done valiantly, but you surpass them all."

Sheker ha-chen, ve-hevel ha- 31:30 *yofi; ishah yirat Adonai, hi tit'halal.*

Charm can mislead, and beauty fades; a woman who fears the LORD is the one to be praised.

T'nu lah mi-pri yadeha, ve- 31:31 *yehal'luha va-she'arim ma'aseha.*

Give her a share of what her hands have produced; let her works bring her praise in the city gates.

The structure of Eshet Chayil:

Eshet Chayil is beautifully nerdy in how it's built, but the basic structure is actually pretty simple:

- **Alphabetical acrostic:**
  It has **22 verses** (Proverbs 31:10–31), one for each letter of the Hebrew alphabet.
  Verse 10 starts with א **(Alef)**, verse 11 with ב **(Bet)**, all the way down to ת **(Tav)**. So it's an A-to-Z portrait of a "woman of valor."

- **Self-contained mini-poems:**
  Each verse is basically a **short couplet or triplet** that can stand on its own. Together, they form a mosaic: wife, businesswoman, mother, merchant, philanthropist, God-fearer.

- **Wisdom poem / heroic hymn:**
  It's written in the style of **Hebrew wisdom poetry**—lots of **parallelism** (second line echoing or deepening the first) and concrete images (wool, flax, ships, vineyards, lamp, loom, city gates).
  The structure moves from:

  - Her **character and worth** (vv. 10–12)

  - Her **work and provision** (vv. 13–24)

  - Her **inner strength and fear of the LORD** (vv. 25–27)

  - The **public praise** she receives (vv. 28–31)

- **Framed by value and praise:**
  It opens with the question, "**Eshet chayil mi yimtza?** – A woman of valor, who can find?" and ends with, "**T'nu lah mi-pri yadeha** – Give her from the fruit of her hands," forming a frame: *who could ever find such a woman?* → *when you do, honor her publicly.*

So structurally: it's an **alphabetic A-to-Z praise song**, wisdom-style, moving from inner character to outward actions to public honor, all anchored in her **yirat Adonai** (fear of the LORD).

Here's a side-by-side look at the first words of each verse so you can *see* the acrostic structure and get the phonetic feel.

Letter	Hebrew (verse start)	Phonetic (approx.)	Verse
א (Alef)	אֵשֶׁת חַיִל מִי יִמְצָא	*Eshet chayil mi yimtza*	31:10
ב (Bet)	בָּטַח בָּהּ לֵב בַּעְלָהּ	*Batach bah lev ba'lah*	31:11
ג (Gimel)	גְּמָלַתְהוּ טוֹב וְלֹא רָע	*Gemalathu tov ve-lo ra*	31:12
ד (Dalet)	דָּרְשָׁה צֶמֶר וּפִשְׁתִּים	*Darshah tzemer u-fishtim*	31:13
ה (He)	הָיְתָה כָּאֳנִיּוֹת סוֹחֵר	*Hayetah ka-oniyot socher*	31:14
ו (Vav)	וַתָּקָם בְּעוֹד לַיְלָה	*Vatakom be'od layla*	31:15
ז (Zayin)	זָמְמָה שָׂדֶה וַתִּקָּחֵהוּ	*Zamemah sadeh va-tikachehu*	31:16
ח (Chet)	חָגְרָה בְעוֹז מָתְנֶיהָ	*Chagra ve-oz motneha*	31:17

ט (Tet)	טָעֲמָה כִּי טוֹב סַחְרָהּ	*Ta'amah ki tov sachrah*	31:18
י (Yod)	יָדֶיהָ שִׁלְּחָה בַכִּישׁוֹר	*Yadeha shilcha ba-kishor*	31:19
כ (Kaf)	כַּפָּהּ פָּרְשָׂה לֶעָנִי	*Kappah parsah le'ani*	31:20
ל (Lamed)	לֹא תִירָא לְבֵיתָהּ מִשָּׁלֶג	*Lo tira le-veitah mi-sheleg*	31:21
מ (Mem)	מַרְבַדִּים עָשְׂתָה לָּהּ	*Marbaddim as'tah lah*	31:22
נ (Nun)	נוֹדָע בַּשְּׁעָרִים בַּעְלָהּ	*Noda ba-she'arim ba'lah*	31:23
ס (Samekh)	סָדִין עָשְׂתָה וַתִּמְכֹּר	*Sadin as'tah va-timkor*	31:24
ע (Ayin)	עֹז וְהָדָר לְבוּשָׁהּ	*Oz ve-hadar levushah*	31:25
פ (Pe)	פִּיהָ פָּתְחָה בְחָכְמָה	*Piha pat'cha be-chokhmah*	31:26
צ (Tsadi)	צוֹפִיָּה הֲלִיכוֹת בֵּיתָהּ	*Tzofiyah halichot beitah*	31:27
ק (Qof)	קָמוּ בָנֶיהָ וַיְאַשְּׁרוּהָ	*Kamu baneha va-ye'ashruha*	31:28
ר (Resh)	רַבּוֹת בָּנוֹת עָשׂוּ חָיִל	*Rabot banot asu chayil*	31:29
שׁ (Shin)	שֶׁקֶר הַחֵן וְהֶבֶל הַיֹּפִי	*Sheker ha-chen ve-hevel ha-yofi*	31:30
ת (Tav)	תְּנוּ־לָהּ מִפְּרִי יָדֶיהָ	*Tenu lah mi-pri yadeha*	31:31

That's the spine of the acrostic: every line stepping through the Hebrew alphabet, praising this **eshet chayil** from א to ת.

THE MEANING OF CHAYIL:

Warrior Strength in Scripture

The first time Scripture pairs the word *chayil* (חַיִל) with a woman is in Proverbs 31:10: "*Eshet Chayil*, who can find? She is more precious than rubies." Many English translations soften the phrase, choosing words like *virtuous, excellent,* or *capable*. Those are not wrong, but they barely skim the surface. Something deeper is happening beneath the Hebrew.

Chayil is not a gentle word. It does not shrink back or hide itself. It carries the sound of strength under pressure, of courage that rises when life is heavy, of someone who does not collapse beneath responsibility. It is a word with movement in it, with muscle and resolve. A word used for armies. A word used for heroes.

If you were to read Proverbs 31 in its original language, you would not come away with the impression of a woman who is fragile or ornamental. You would sense steadiness. Presence. A life marked by discernment and grit, by hands that work and a heart that stands firm. The beauty of *Eshet Chayil* is not found in perfection. It is found in strength.

A Word with a Warrior's History

To understand what the writer of Proverbs is doing here, it helps to notice how Scripture uses *chayil* elsewhere. The pattern is unmistakable.

When the angel of the Lord appears to Gideon in Judges 6, he greets him as *gibor chayil*—a mighty warrior. When King Saul's servants describe the young David in 1 Samuel 16, they call him an *ish chayil*, a man of valor. In other places, the word describes armies, military strength, and the capacity of a leader to remain steady under pressure.

Again and again, *chayil* points to resilience. Strength with purpose. Courage joined to character.

So when Proverbs 31 uses this word to describe a woman, it is not speaking of someone who is morally tidy or quietly impressive. It is naming spiritual substance. This is not a decorative role. It is a dignified one. Not a trinket to admire, but a life of weight and presence.

So often, women are handed ideals of perfection rather than ideals of strength. The Hebrew text gently but firmly pushes back. It calls women toward courage, wholeness, resilience, faithfulness, and a life deeply rooted in God.

The Strength of Presence, Not Performance

One of the most surprising things about *chayil* is that it is never about impressing others. It is about standing. Standing in faith. Standing in truth. Standing in God's purposes, even when those purposes unfold slowly.

It shows up in the mother who refuses to let hope die.
In the young woman who chooses integrity when compromise would be easier.
In the leader who speaks with wisdom rather than bravado.
In the older woman whose calm faith steadies an entire family.

This is not performance-based strength.
It is presence-based strength.

Valor begins in the inner life. Faith, character, discipline, courage—
these are the places where strength takes root. The actions
described in Proverbs 31 flow naturally from a heart shaped over
time by God's presence.

Strength That Looks Different in Every Woman

One of the most freeing truths about *chayil* is that it does not look
the same in every life. Valor is not tied to personality, gifting, or
stage of life. It emerges in the choices a woman makes, often quietly,
day by day.

In Ruth, *chayil* looks like loyalty and courageous love.
In Deborah, it looks like wisdom and steady leadership.
In Hannah, it looks like perseverance in prayer.
In Sarah, it looks like hope that matures with time.

Strength wears many faces. Yet the root is always the same: trust in
God.

Why This Word Matters

Proverbs closes with this poem intentionally. It is a culmination.
Throughout the book, wisdom is described as something to pursue,
to cherish, to embody. Then, at the very end, the writer offers a
living picture.

Here is wisdom made visible.
Here is what it looks like when a life is aligned with God.

The Woman of Valor is wisdom walking around in real life. Her
strength is not theoretical. It is lived. Practiced. Possible.

This is part of why the poem is written as an acrostic, each line
beginning with a different letter of the Hebrew alphabet. It is a way
of saying her life reflects wisdom from beginning to end. Not a

checklist to complete, but a portrait to behold. Not a model to copy line by line, but a vision that inspires courage.

Strength Rooted in God

In the end, *chayil* is not a pressure word. It is a promise word. It speaks to what God cultivates in a woman who seeks Him. Strength that grows from worship. Courage that develops through trust. Wisdom shaped by daily faithfulness.

This strength does not demand perfection. It invites growth.
It does not elevate flawless behavior. It honors God's presence at work in an ordinary life.
It does not confine women to narrow roles. It dignifies their full humanity, gifting, and purpose.

When Scripture calls a woman *Eshet Chayil*, it names what God already sees—a warrior heart, formed by His love, steadied by His truth, and ready for whatever season comes next.

This book is an exploration of that formation. Before we meet Ruth, Hannah, Deborah, and Sarah, we begin here, with the foundation: valor is not something you earn. It is something God forms within you.

So for now, pause.
Let the word settle.
Let its weight rest gently, not heavily.

Chayil.
Strength.
Courage.
Valor.

It belongs to you more than you may realize.

REFLECTIONS

Strength does not always announce itself. Often, it hides in everyday faithfulness—in the way you keep showing up, in the way you quietly refuse to abandon something God placed in your care. It may appear in how you navigate responsibility, in how you recover after disappointment, or in how you choose honesty when silence would be simpler.

As you think through the rhythm of your days, notice where patience rises when frustration would be quicker, where kindness is offered without recognition, and where clarity or boundaries now come more naturally than they once did. These small, uncelebrated choices are often the clearest signs that *chayil* is already alive in you. Recognizing them helps you see that valor is not a distant goal. It is already at work.

Different aspects of *chayil* resonate with different seasons. Strength may speak to you if you have carried weight for a long time or served as a quiet backbone for others. Courage may stir if you are standing at the edge of uncertainty or facing decisions that require bravery. Capability may surface as you step into new roles or responsibilities. Excellence may resonate if you are learning to offer your best without chasing perfection.

Pay attention to which word stirs something in you—comfort, longing, recognition, or even resistance. That response may be a gentle invitation from the Spirit, pointing toward the place where God is shaping something deeper within you.

Many women also carry expectations that did not originate in Scripture—expectations to manage everything flawlessly, to hold emotions steady, to achieve more while resting less, or to mirror someone else's calling instead of honoring their own. Some of these pressures come from culture or community. Others rise from quiet inner narratives about what makes us valuable or worthy of love.

It may be worth asking what expectations you have carried that no longer serve you. Which align with God's vision, and which weigh you down unnecessarily? What might change if you released the need to appear strong and allowed God to form true strength instead? Letting go of false measures is often part of becoming a Woman of Valor. As that weight lifts, the strength God gives becomes clearer.

Finally, consider where God may be inviting you to grow stronger right now. Growth rarely arrives all at once. It unfolds slowly, in places where God nudges gently. He may be strengthening your faith through waiting, your wisdom through decision-making, your courage through new doors that feel intimidating, or your kindness through relationships that stretch you.

Strength forms where God meets your real life, not an idealized one. The places that feel tender, resistant, or quietly uncomfortable may be the very places where *chayil* is taking root.

IDENTITY BEFORE ACTIVITY:

Who You Are Matters More Than What You Do

Before Proverbs 31 describes anything the Woman of Valor does, it begins with who she is. That distinction is easy to miss, especially for modern readers. We tend to move quickly to the list of activities—providing food, managing a household, investing wisely, caring for the poor—and treat them as markers of spiritual success.

But Scripture works in the opposite direction.

Actions never create identity.
Identity gives rise to action.

What you do flows from who you are.
What you build reflects what is already being formed within you.

This chapter is a quiet turning point in the book. Before we speak about Ruth's courage, Hannah's devotion, Deborah's leadership, or Sarah's endurance, we pause here. We look inward. We ask what it means to be a woman whose life is anchored in God before anything is accomplished.

The world ties identity to performance. Scripture ties identity to presence—God's presence within a woman, shaping her into someone steady, rooted, and whole. That difference changes everything.

The Inner Life: Where Strength Begins

Proverbs 31 opens with a question: *"Eshet Chayil*, who can find?" This is not a lament about scarcity, as though strong women are rare or elusive. It is an invitation to look deeper. Strength like this is precious because it is cultivated. It grows slowly, formed over time, shaped from the inside out.

The poem moves outward from identity, not inward from ability. The woman described is not striving to impress. She is living from a centered place.

In Scripture, the heart is the seat of direction and devotion. What forms there eventually shapes everything else. A strong inner life does not announce itself loudly, but it carries certain markers—clarity where there was once confusion, conviction where fear once ruled, purpose where drifting once felt normal, integrity where image once mattered more, faithfulness where frenzy once dominated.

A woman of valor does not chase strength. She grows it. And growth always begins with identity.

How Identity Gets Misplaced

It is surprisingly easy to lose yourself in what you do. Many women collapse identity into roles—mother, wife, daughter, leader, caregiver, helper, problem-solver. These roles can be meaningful and even sacred, but they were never meant to bear the full weight of a woman's sense of self.

Roles shift.
Responsibilities change.
Seasons reshape us.

When identity rests on accomplishment alone, it becomes fragile. A change in circumstance can leave a woman feeling unsteady or unsure of who she is. Proverbs consistently warns against building life on foundations that cannot hold.

When God shapes identity, He builds something sturdier. You are valued because He calls you His. You are strong because He forms strength within you. You are a Woman of Valor not because you meet a standard, but because God is at work shaping you.

Identity must be rooted in what cannot be taken away.

Identity Rooted in God's Vision

From the beginning of Scripture to its closing pages, God's vision for women is expansive. It includes partnership and leadership, creativity and nurture, discernment and spiritual authority. The biblical story is filled with women who lead, protect, teach, comfort, persevere, and shape the future in quiet and bold ways alike.

The Woman of Valor poem is not a cage. It is a window. It offers a glimpse of what a woman becomes when her identity is held firmly in God's hands.

When identity is rooted in Him, certain qualities begin to emerge naturally—steadiness in uncertainty, calm in chaos, courage in calling, wisdom in decisions, kindness in relationships, perseverance in struggle. As these take shape within, the outer life reflects them in diverse and meaningful ways.

This is why Proverbs 31 describes such a wide range of activity. Strength expressed through identity is flexible. It adapts to the season. It meets real life where it is.

Reclaiming Identity from Expectations

Every woman carries expectations, often quietly. Some were spoken aloud. Others were absorbed over time. Expectations about how much to carry, how little to need, how well to manage, how perfectly to perform.

Comparison whispers that you should be more like someone else.
Fear cautions against taking risks.
Shame insists you are not enough.
Pride tells you to do everything alone.
Weariness suggests you have nothing left to give.

Against those voices, God speaks differently. He reminds you that you are His, that He is with you, that He is forming you patiently, and that strength is already growing within you.

As false expectations loosen their grip, something steadier emerges. Identity settles where it belongs—not in pressure, but in truth.

What Identity Sounds Like in Real Life

Identity has a voice. It shapes decisions long before they become visible actions. A woman grounded in who God says she is begins to speak differently, even to herself.

She can rest without guilt.
She can speak truth with kindness and clarity.
She can step into opportunity without fear.
She can say no when necessary.
She can release the need to please everyone.
She can refuse to be defined by past mistakes or future uncertainty.

Strength begins here—not in activity, but in awareness. When a woman understands who she is, she begins to understand what she is called to do.

This is *chayil* before it can be seen.

REFLECTIONS

Many women discover that their sense of identity has quietly
wrapped itself around their responsibilities. Caregiving,
productivity, leadership, problem-solving—these can all become
places where worth is measured. Yet responsibilities are seasonal.
They change as life changes. When identity leans too heavily on
what you do, it can feel fragile when circumstances shift.

It may help to name the roles you carry and notice which ones feel
tied to your sense of value. There is no need for judgment here.
Awareness itself is a step toward a deeper foundation—one that
remains steady even when life rearranges itself.

Transitions often reveal more than routines. When responsibilities
increase, do you feel pressure to prove yourself? When they
decrease, do you feel unseen or unnecessary? When rest appears,
does guilt follow close behind? These responses are not failures.
They are clues. They show where God may be gently reshaping the
inner structure of your life so that identity rests in Him rather than
in performance.

Expectations also play a powerful role. Some expectations come
from family or culture. Others rise from faith communities or from
our own inner narratives. They may tell you to hold everything
together, to never falter, to anticipate everyone's needs, or to remain
endlessly capable. It can be healing to ask where those expectations
came from and whether they align with how God sees you.

Releasing what does not belong to you creates space for what does.

Finally, notice which truth about your identity in God feels hardest
to believe. Perhaps it is the idea that you are already enough, or that

God's approval is not earned, or that rest is not weakness. Resistance often signals that a truth is touching a tender place, one still learning to trust.

God works patiently. He rebuilds what pressure and fear have shaped, restoring a sense of self that is rooted, resilient, and quietly strong. Over time, strength begins to feel less like something you strive for and more like something that grows naturally within you.

RUTH:

Strength in Young Adulthood

Strength does not always announce itself. It does not always arrive with authority or experience. Sometimes it enters quietly, through the life of someone who feels exposed and uncertain—a young widow far from home, with no resources, no security, and no clear path forward.

Ruth steps into Scripture without title or protection, without advantage or influence. Yet the book that bears her name offers one of the clearest pictures of *chayil*—valor, fortitude, and inner resolve—formed in the early years of adulthood.

Young adulthood is often a season of transition. The ground is still shifting beneath your feet. Decisions feel weighty. The future feels both open and fragile at the same time. Ruth's story speaks directly into this space because she is asked a defining question long before she knows how her life will unfold:

Who will I be when everything familiar falls away?

Her answer becomes the foundation of her strength.

The Faithfulness That Redefined Her Future

Ruth's story opens with loss. She loses her husband, her home, and the world she knew. Standing beside Naomi, she is urged to return to what is familiar and safe. No one would have faulted her for doing so.

Instead, Ruth makes a different choice—one rooted not in self-preservation, but in character.

> *"Where you go, I will go… your people will be my people, and your God my God."*

In Hebrew, these words carry the weight of covenant. They are not emotional promises spoken in the heat of the moment. They are language of allegiance, loyalty, and long-term commitment. Ruth is not pressured into this vow. She is not bound by obligation. She chooses it freely, guided by conviction.

Ruth's first act of valor is faithfulness. She chooses commitment when retreat would have been easier. That single decision quietly sets the direction of her entire life.

Young adulthood often asks similar questions, even if they arrive more subtly. Who will shape my values? What will guide my choices? What kind of person am I becoming? Ruth's story reminds us that strength often begins with clarity of allegiance—to God and to the people He places in our lives.

The Courage to Step Into the Unknown

Following Naomi to Bethlehem was not a romantic adventure. It was an act of courage. Ruth stepped into a land where she was a foreigner, without economic security, legal protection, or social standing. She faced cultural barriers and daily vulnerability, yet she moved forward with quiet resolve.

This is often what courage looks like in young adulthood. Not dramatic or loud, but steady. The courage to begin again. The courage to trust God with a future that cannot yet be seen. The courage to rebuild when certainty has disappeared.

Ruth's uncertainty is not a sign of weakness. It is the soil where her strength grows.

Work as an Expression of Faith

When Ruth arrives in Bethlehem, she does not wait for rescue. She goes to the fields to glean—humble work, reserved for those with few options. She asks permission. She works long hours. She provides for Naomi with care and dignity.

Boaz notices her, not for appearance or status, but for character.

> *"All that you have done… has been fully reported to me."*

Later, he names what others already see: "All the people of my town know that you are an **Eshet Chayil**—a Woman of Valor."

This matters. Ruth is called a Woman of Valor before marriage, before motherhood, before visible reward. She is honored for who she is—faithful, diligent, steady, and kind.

In a culture that often pressures young adults to prove worth through achievement or independence, Ruth offers another vision. Her strength is revealed through perseverance, humility, and responsibility. Work becomes an act of worship. Faithfulness becomes a way of protecting others. Service becomes a quiet expression of devotion.

These, too, are forms of strength.

God at Work in the Quiet Details

Ruth's life changes in ways she could never have orchestrated. Provision comes. Protection follows. Redemption unfolds. Yet none of it happens quickly. God works in the ordinary days—the repetitive ones, the days that feel unseen and unremarkable.

Strength in young adulthood is often formed in these very spaces. In showing up again and again. In routines that feel small. In patience that stretches. In the willingness to begin at the bottom without resentment.

These are not wasted seasons. They are formative ones.

Ruth likely believed she was simply gathering grain. In reality, she was stepping into a story far larger than she could imagine—a lineage that would lead to King David, and ultimately to the Messiah.

Faithfulness in small things shapes futures we cannot yet see.

REFLECTIONS

Most lives include crossroads—moments when the next step feels unclear and the weight of choice settles in. Some crossroads are relational, others financial, emotional, or spiritual. Ruth's story invites you to notice where decision-making feels heavy right now and to gently ask what is guiding your choices. Is it fear, comfort, expectation, or conviction? Often, the strength God is forming becomes most visible at these points of transition.

Courage also deserves to be named when it appears quietly. It may show up in leaving something unhealthy, standing beside someone in pain, or choosing to begin again after loss. You may have shown bravery without recognizing it as such. Taking time to acknowledge these moments helps you see where *chayil*—valor—is already present in your life.

Uncertainty has a way of shaping faith. When the future feels undefined, emotions often surface—anxiety, hope, fatigue, or anticipation. None of these disqualify you. God's guidance is active even when clarity is not. Paying attention to how uncertainty is forming you may reveal where God is inviting deeper trust.

Finally, consider the ordinary responsibilities of your days. Ruth's strength was revealed through steady work and quiet faithfulness. Studying, caring for others, building a career, managing a household—these spaces often feel unremarkable, yet they are where God frequently forms resilience and character. It may be worth asking where strength is being shaped in the everyday rhythms of your own life.

HANNAH:

Strength in Motherhood &
Family Life

Motherhood—whether experienced, hoped for, spiritual, or symbolic—is one of the most emotionally layered callings in a woman's life. It can hold joy and exhaustion, fulfillment and longing, deep gratitude and deep grief all at once. Scripture does not shy away from this complexity. Instead, it introduces us to Hannah, a woman whose strength takes shape through persistent faith.

Before she is known as Samuel's mother, Hannah is known as a woman who prays through pain. There are no shortcuts in her story and no instant resolution. She lives through a long season of waiting—waiting with honesty, waiting with endurance, waiting with a hope that refuses to disappear.

Through her, we encounter a different expression of *chayil*: strength that kneels, strength that weeps, and strength that continues to show up before God.

A Season Marked by Longing

Hannah's story opens in 1 Samuel with a longing that cuts deep. She desires a child she does not have. In the ancient world, infertility carried social weight and quiet shame. Women were often judged by measures God never used, and Hannah carries that burden year after year.

Her pain is sharpened by the presence of a rival wife who mocks and provokes her repeatedly. Peninnah's words reopen wounds that never quite have time to heal. Hannah's husband, Elkanah, loves her and tries to comfort her, but even sincere affection cannot remove the ache.

Some seasons of life feel like this—longing unfulfilled, pressure applied by outside voices, and pain too deep to be soothed by well-meaning reassurance. Scripture does not rush Hannah past this place. It names her sorrow and allows it to stand.

The story does not avoid grief.
It moves through it.

Valor is faith that remains present within sorrow.

Strength That Prays Through Pain

Hannah's turning point comes when she goes to the Tabernacle and pours out her soul before God, long before her circumstances change. Her prayer is not polished or restrained. It is raw, honest, and unguarded.

> *"I am a woman deeply troubled… I have been pouring out my soul before the Lord."*

This is one of Scripture's clearest pictures of prayer—not carefully constructed words, but a heart laid bare. Hannah does not pretend to be strong. She does not minimize her disappointment. She brings every emotion into God's presence.

Her valor is not found in holding herself together.
It is found in trusting God with what she cannot.

Sometimes strength sounds like a trembling voice that still chooses to pray.

A Vow Shaped by Devotion

In her anguish, Hannah makes a vow. If God grants her a son, she will dedicate him entirely to the service of the Lord. This is not a bargain struck in desperation. It is an act of devotion. Hannah offers back to God the very thing she longs for most.

Here, *chayil* takes another form.
It is the strength to surrender what you love.
The strength to release what you cannot control.
The strength to trust God with the future of someone entrusted to you.

When Samuel is born and later weaned, Hannah fulfills her vow with quiet resolve. She brings him to the Tabernacle and places him in God's care, saying simply,

> ***"I prayed for this child, and the Lord has granted me what I asked."***

Her motherhood becomes both nurturing and surrender.
Care and release held together.

There is a holy resilience in her.

The Song of a Woman of Valor

After releasing her son, Hannah does something unexpected—she sings. Her song in 1 Samuel 2 is one of the earliest and most theologically rich hymns in Scripture. It speaks of God's justice, His power to reverse circumstances, and His faithfulness to the humble.

Her words echo across generations, shaping Mary's song centuries later. Hannah emerges not only as a mother, but as a theologian and a prophetic voice. Her understanding of God deepens through suffering, and her faith becomes something that blesses far beyond her own life.

Strength in motherhood—literal or spiritual—nurtures life. It also declares truth, carries hope, and passes faith forward.

Hannah is a Woman of Valor not because she mothers without flaw, but because she anchors her motherhood in God.

Strength in Family Life Today

Family life today carries no less complexity. Women hold emotional and relational weight—caring, coordinating, protecting, nurturing, navigating conflict, and tending their own inner lives alongside the needs of others.

Hannah's story offers a gentle pattern rather than a prescription. Honest prayer. Steady perseverance. Willing surrender. And joy that grows out of trust rather than certainty.

Her strength is shaped in communion with God.

Motherhood—biological or spiritual—is sacred work. Hannah's journey reminds every woman who carries others in her heart that she is not carrying them alone.

REFLECTIONS

Longing often lingers quietly in the background of life. It may be a desire for family, healing, reconciliation, or a future that has not yet opened. Hannah's story invites you to notice where longing lives in you now and to bring it honestly before God, without apology or shame. Strength often begins where unmet desire is entrusted to Him.

Many women learn to hide emotions that feel too raw—disappointment, grief, fear, even hope. Hannah shows that vulnerability is not a weakness of faith. It is often the doorway to deeper trust. The feelings you suppress may be the very places where God longs to meet you with comfort or clarity.

There may also be something God is inviting you to surrender—not as defeat, but as trust. Surrender does not mean letting go of love. It means loosening the grip of control and allowing God to hold what matters most alongside you. This kind of release is not loss; it is faith practiced in real time.

As you reflect on difficult seasons in your own story, consider how they may have shaped compassion, resilience, or wisdom within you. Hardship does not leave us unchanged. Like a chick breaking through its shell, persistence builds strength alongside new life. Waiting can form patience. Loss can deepen empathy. These quiet transformations are often the clearest signs of *chayil* taking root in the inner life.

DEBORAH:

*Strength in Midlife &
Leadership*

If Ruth shows us strength in young adulthood and Hannah shows us strength formed in the tender places of family life, Deborah stands before us as a woman whose strength has matured. Her story reflects the richness of midlife—a season when experience deepens, discernment sharpens, and influence begins to take shape in ways that earlier years could not have predicted.

Deborah enters the story of Judges with striking clarity. She is not introduced by lineage or domestic role, but by calling: a prophetess who is judging Israel during a time of instability and oppression. Her authority is evident, and her leadership is grounded. She speaks and people listen, not because she demands attention, but because her wisdom carries weight.

Midlife often carries this same quality. It is a season when women begin to recognize the reach of their influence and the value of what has been shaped through years of walking with God. Deborah stands as a witness that this kind of maturity is not something to be hidden or diminished. It is a form of *chayil*—valor tested by time and strengthened through faithfulness.

A Leader Formed by Listening

Before Deborah leads a nation or calls a general to action, she listens. Scripture places her beneath a palm tree, an image of steadiness and accessibility. People come to her for counsel, and she offers discernment shaped by attentiveness—to God, to people, and to the moment they are living in.

This is not the wisdom of haste or impulse. It is the wisdom of seasons. It grows through watching, waiting, and allowing God to form understanding slowly. Deborah's leadership flows from spiritual sensitivity rather than force.

Strength in midlife often carries this same quiet clarity. It emerges from years of paying attention, from learning when to speak and when to wait, from understanding that wisdom is formed as much by listening as by acting.

Calling Others into Courage

One of the most compelling aspects of Deborah's leadership is the way she draws courage out of others. When Israel faces oppression under Sisera, God instructs Deborah to summon Barak. She delivers God's word clearly, calling him to step into a role that requires bravery.

Barak hesitates. He asks Deborah to go with him.

Rather than shaming him, Deborah stands alongside him. She agrees to go, not as a warrior wielding a weapon, but as a spiritual presence—a steady companion who strengthens resolve rather than replacing it.

Deborah's valor is not expressed through domination or control. It is revealed in her ability to call courage forward in someone else.

This is often what leadership looks like in midlife. Mentoring. Encouraging. Offering steadiness when others feel unsure. Providing clarity without taking over. A Woman of Valor does not hoard her strength; she cultivates it in those around her.

Strength Rooted in Partnership with God

Deborah understands that victory does not belong to human strategy alone. Her confidence is anchored in God's presence rather than her own authority. When the moment comes, she speaks not as a general, but as a prophetess, reminding Barak that the outcome rests in God's hands.

Her leadership is collaborative. She takes her place, but she never attempts to take God's place.

This distinction matters deeply for women who lead today. Strength does not require self-promotion. Authority does not demand dominance. Influence does not depend on volume.

Deborah models leadership that is confident and bold, yet deeply humble. She knows who she is, and she knows where her strength comes from.

A Legacy That Sings

After the victory, Deborah does something unexpected. She sings. Judges 5 records her song—a poetic retelling of deliverance that honors God and acknowledges the courage of those who stepped forward.

In midlife, many women carry years of unseen labor, quiet perseverance, and victories that were never publicly named. Deborah's song reminds us that these stories matter. Strength deserves to be remembered, gratitude deserves a voice, and faith deserves to be spoken aloud.

Deborah's legacy is not only one of leadership, but of worship and truth. Her strength blesses others and builds something that lasts.

This is *chayil* in its mature form—strength that guides, steadies, and leaves behind a faithful imprint.

REFLECTIONS

Wisdom rarely arrives all at once. It forms through years of living—through mistakes and resilience, forgiveness and reflection, learning when to speak and when to remain silent. As you look back over your life, notice how your understanding has changed. The way you make decisions, read situations, and listen to others has likely been shaped by God more than you realize.

Many women offer strength without naming it as such. You may find yourself steadying someone else's emotions, helping them think clearly, or offering encouragement at just the right moment. Influence often appears in ordinary conversations rather than formal roles. Paying attention to these moments helps you recognize the quiet reach of your presence.

Leadership can surface in many spaces—family, work, community, or congregation. God's invitation to lead often carries both humility and confidence. It is not about control, but about guidance. Not about proving yourself, but about serving with clarity and courage.

Legacy is built slowly. It forms through consistent choices, faithful words, and a life lived before God. Consider the people your life touches. What strength do they draw from you? What steadiness remains when you step away? These are the lasting marks of *chayil*—valor lived out in ways that extend far beyond a single season.

SARAH:

Strength in Later Years

There is a particular kind of strength that often emerges only with time. It is shaped by long seasons of waiting, by years of experience, and by the slow, steady maturing of faith. This strength does not rush. It does not panic. It has learned—sometimes painfully—that God often works on a timeline far longer, and far wiser, than our own.

Sarah embodies this form of *chayil*. She enters the biblical story as a woman of significance and partnership, walking alongside Abraham into a calling that would shape generations. Yet her journey unfolds gradually. She becomes a matriarch, but not all at once. Her valor forms across years marked by laughter and doubt, frustration and hope, weariness and transformation.

If Deborah reflects the strength of mature leadership, Sarah reveals the strength of mature faith.

A Calling That Requires Waiting

From the beginning, Sarah is woven into God's promise to Abraham. When God declares that Abraham will become the father of many nations, Sarah stands beside him as part of that future. Yet the years stretch on, and nothing seems to change. Their life is filled with movement—tents, journeys, famine, danger, uncertainty—yet still no child.

Scripture does not rush past Sarah's struggle. It allows her disappointment to be seen. She wrestles with the tension between what God has spoken and what she experiences day after day. Waiting becomes a defining landscape of her life.

For many women, later seasons carry similar terrain. There is the reckoning with prayers that took longer than expected, the revisiting of choices made long ago, the arrival of a quieter perspective shaped by experience. Often, there is also a deeper awareness of God's presence, even when some questions remain unanswered.

Waiting becomes its own teacher.
Not because it is gentle, but because it reveals where trust is being formed.

Valor often takes shape in these long spaces, where dependence on God is tested and refined.

Faith That Learns to Laugh Again

One of the most intimate moments in Sarah's story comes when visitors arrive at Abraham's tent and announce that she will bear a son. Sarah listens from behind the tent—part hidden, part curious, part guarded. When she hears the promise, she laughs.

It is not a laugh of mockery, but of someone who has lived with disappointment long enough to protect herself from hope. God hears her laughter and responds with a question that is both gentle and piercing: "Is anything too wonderful for the Lord?"

Later, when Isaac is born, Sarah laughs again. This time, the laughter is different. It carries joy, astonishment, relief, and gratitude.

Here is one of the quiet beauties of strength in later years. God does not erase pain by pretending it never existed. He redeems it. He transforms guarded laughter into joy, not by denying weariness, but by meeting it with faithfulness.

Sarah's story teaches us that mature faith often holds a kind of holy laughter—an awareness that God's goodness extends far beyond our timelines, our exhaustion, and our expectations.

Wisdom Shaped by Long Roads

Sarah's life was complex and, at times, deeply painful. She lived through migration and famine, through moments of courage and moments of fear. She experienced conflict, loss, and vulnerability, and she walked beside Abraham through both faithfulness and failure.

These experiences shaped a woman who understood both the fragility and the endurance of faith. Her wisdom was not theoretical. It was earned through perseverance.

Women in later seasons often carry this kind of wisdom. They have lived long enough to recognize patterns, to discern which battles matter, and to understand the cost of bitterness. They know the value of gentleness and the difference between urgency and importance.

This is *chayil* in its reflective form—strength expressed through clarity, patience, and spiritual steadiness.

A Legacy Rooted in Promise

Sarah's influence extends far beyond her lifetime. She becomes the mother of Isaac, the matriarch of Israel, and part of the unfolding promise through which God would bless the world. Scripture does not hide her humanity or her missteps. Her legacy rests not on flawlessness, but on God's faithfulness and her eventual trust in that faithfulness.

Later years offer women a sacred opportunity to shape legacy with intention. This often happens quietly—through the stories they share, the prayers they carry, the wisdom they pass along, and the blessing they speak over younger generations. Stability offered in uncertain times becomes a gift that endures.

Legacy is not only what remains after we are gone.
It is what we build into others while we are still here.

Sarah's story reminds us that legacy forms slowly, through decades of walking with God and allowing Him to shape both the heart and the horizon.

REFLECTIONS

Some promises unfold far more slowly than we expect. Delayed hope can feel especially heavy in later seasons, when time itself feels more precious. It may help to reflect on the prayers or longings that have lingered for years rather than weeks. Waiting may have been painful, but it has not been empty. Notice how endurance, perspective, and faithfulness have taken shape along the way.

Faith often changes as the years pass. Early faith may lean toward certainty, while later faith rests more deeply in trust. Consider how your relationship with God has matured—how your prayers sound now, how patience has stretched you, how wisdom has softened or strengthened your heart.

There may also be places where joy feels distant. Sarah's laughter did not disappear forever; it was transformed. Reflect on where hope has grown fragile or where joy has faded under the weight of disappointment. These tender places may be where God is gently inviting restoration, wonder, and new life.

Finally, consider the legacy you are shaping. Legacy reaches beyond family lines. It includes spiritual daughters and sons, friendships, communities, and all those touched by your life. Faith, wisdom, resilience, and courage are gifts that ripple outward long after words are forgotten. These, too, are marks of *chayil*—strength formed over time and offered generously to others.

FAITH:

The First Root of Strength

Faith is the first root of *chayil*—the inner anchor that steadies a woman in every season. Long before strength becomes visible in action, it takes shape quietly, deep within the places where you meet God when no one else is watching. Outward courage grows from inward trust. Wisdom begins with reverence. And true valor is formed through a faith that keeps reaching for God even when circumstances shift or hope arrives slowly.

Faith does not require the absence of fear. It does not demand flawless prayers or unwavering confidence. Faithful people still doubt. Still struggle. Still wrestle.

Yet faith carries a steadiness to it. It is the quiet assurance of God's presence shaping your perspective, calming your spirit, and giving you strength beyond what you could manufacture on your own. The Woman of Valor described in Proverbs 31 lives from this deep well. Her actions carry purpose because her confidence is grounded. Her diligence endures because her hope is rooted. She stands firm not by sheer willpower, but by a practiced trust in the character of God.

This chapter is an invitation to notice how that trust is formed.

Faith as Daily Dependence

Faith is often imagined as something that shows up only in dramatic moments—during crisis, loss, or visible miracles. But the faith that forms *chayil* is shaped slowly, through daily dependence rather than occasional inspiration.

It looks like prayer offered when the mind is clear and when it is tired.
It looks like Scripture opened when understanding feels strong and when nothing seems to land.
It looks like seeking God not only in desperation, but also in gratitude.

Faith is not a feeling to wait for. It is a relationship to tend.

Over time, dependence grows as you learn—sometimes through difficulty—that God remains steady when you are not, faithful when circumstances confuse you, and present even when you feel alone. This kind of trust rests not in outcomes, but in who God is.

This is the quiet courage at the root of *chayil*. Faith that is practiced, not theoretical.

Faith That Walks Through Uncertainty

Every woman encounters seasons where the way forward is unclear. Ruth knew this. Hannah lived it. Deborah and Sarah carried it as well. Uncertainty touches every life.

What differs is not the presence of uncertainty, but how a woman learns to walk within it.

Faith grows in uncertain seasons not by scrambling for answers, but by remaining rooted. When life feels unpredictable, faith teaches us to pause, to breathe, and to seek God's presence before seeking solutions. It reminds us that walking with God matters more than knowing every step ahead.

This trust reshapes how difficulties are carried. Faith offers resilience that often surprises us. It nurtures hope that revives rather than pressures. It gives courage to continue even when outcomes remain unseen.

This is a defining mark of *chayil*: the ability to face the unknown with quiet steadiness grounded in confidence that God is near.

Faith That Holds Joy and Sorrow Together

Mature faith is spacious. It can hold grief and gratitude at the same time. It understands that life rarely moves in straight lines and that seasons are often layered—bright and shadowed, hopeful and heavy, all at once.

This kind of faith allows honest prayer without losing hope. It allows lament without collapse. It gives permission to rejoice without pretending everything is resolved. Faith becomes the place where you bring your whole self—strength and weakness, expectation and disappointment—and discover that God meets you there with compassion.

Many women carry emotional weight for others—children, partners, families, friends, communities. Faith becomes the place where those burdens are released, even if only a little at a time. It becomes the space where you remember that you were never meant to hold everything together on your own.

Strength is not found in carrying everything.
It is found in knowing where to set things down.

Faith Expressed Through Obedience

Faith naturally expresses itself through obedience—not as rigid rule-keeping, but as daily alignment with God's voice. Over time, faith shapes small choices that form character.

Integrity is chosen when shortcuts whisper.
Kindness is offered when irritation rises.
Truth is spoken when silence feels safer.
Generosity is practiced when self-protection calls loudly.
Forgiveness is extended when resentment tries to take hold.

As these choices repeat, obedience becomes less about discipline
and more about harmony—your heart gradually aligning with God's
wisdom. This is why faith sits at the foundation of strength. It
prepares the ground for every other virtue to grow.

Faith That Trusts the Long Story

God rarely works quickly. Scripture unfolds slowly—through years
of wandering, generations of waiting, long stretches between
promise and fulfillment. Faith teaches us to lift our eyes beyond the
moment and remember that God's story for a life is larger than any
single chapter.

A faithful woman learns, over time, to release her timeline and lean
into God's. She begins to recognize that delays and detours are often
part of preparation, and that unseen seasons may be doing deeper
work than visible success ever could.

This long view of faith brings humility and steadiness. It reminds us
that God's work within us is ongoing, and that the story He is writing
is more faithful and beautiful than anything we could script on our
own.

REFLECTIONS

Trust often grows in the places that feel uncertain or stretched. It
may help to notice where anxiety or hesitation lingers in your life
right now. These places are not failures of faith. They are often

invitations—gentle openings where God is drawing you toward deeper trust and steadier reliance on Him.

Faith also changes with time. Looking back at earlier seasons may reveal how your understanding of God has matured. Perhaps certainty has given way to endurance, or emotion has softened into steadiness. These shifts are signs of growth, shaped by years of walking with God.

Daily rhythms quietly nourish faith. Prayer, Scripture, reflection, gratitude—these practices anchor the heart over time. It may be worth asking which rhythms steady you now, and whether God is inviting you into something new or renewed in this season.

Memory, too, can strengthen trust. Recalling moments when God met you in difficulty or guided you through confusion can offer courage for the present. The God who was faithful then has not changed. He walks with you still.

WISDOM:

Clear Sight for the Journey

Wisdom is one of the most defining qualities of a Woman of Valor. If faith anchors her heart, wisdom guides her steps. It shapes how she understands herself, how she reads situations, how she responds to others, and how she notices the quiet fingerprints of God woven through both the ordinary and the unexpected.

Wisdom is more than information gathered or insight accumulated. It is perception refined over time. It is discernment shaped by Scripture and clarified through intimacy with God. Wisdom does not rush to conclusions. It sees with patience, listens with care, and moves with intention.

In the Hebrew Scriptures, wisdom—***chokhma*** (חָכְמָה)—carries the sense of skill as much as insight. It is the ability to build well, to choose well, to live well. Wisdom is not abstract. It is lived. It is the steady shaping of a life that reflects God's character.

A woman who cultivates wisdom begins to see differently. She notices what lies beneath the surface. She recognizes patterns others miss. She senses when it is time to move forward and when waiting is the wiser path. She listens more than she reacts, and when she speaks, her words carry weight.

Wisdom becomes her lamp—not blinding, not hurried, but sufficient for the next step.

Wisdom Begins with Reverence

Scripture is clear that wisdom begins with reverence for God. This reverence is not fear of God's punishment, but awe rooted in trust in our God. It is the recognition that God sees what we cannot see and knows what we do not yet understand.

Reverence slows the soul. It shifts attention away from impulse and toward alignment. The question changes—from *What do I want right now?* to *What reflects God's heart?*

This posture of humility becomes the soil where wisdom grows.

A Woman of Valor is not wise because she has all the answers. She is wise because she knows where to seek them. Wisdom begins with listening—listening to Scripture, listening to God's Spirit, and listening honestly to the experiences that have shaped her life.

Wisdom That Discerns Paths and People

Life is filled with crossroads, many of them unmarked. Wisdom helps interpret the terrain. Some paths look easy but slowly drain the soul. Others demand sacrifice yet lead to growth and depth. Wisdom learns to look beyond what is immediate and consider what will endure.

Rather than reacting, wisdom pauses. It weighs direction, consequence, and alignment. It asks not only whether a choice feels right, but whether it shapes character, deepens peace, and draws the heart closer to God.

Wisdom also sharpens how a woman reads people. It helps her distinguish sincerity from flattery, truth from confusion, health from harm. It guides her toward relationships that nourish life and gives her the clarity to set boundaries when needed.

A wise woman is not suspicious—she is perceptive.
She is not guarded—she is discerning.
She is not distant—she is intentional.

This clarity protects her and allows her strength to be used wisely.

Wisdom in Words

Scripture often links wisdom with speech, because words carry great power. They can heal or wound, steady or unsettle, restore or divide. A woman who cultivates wisdom becomes attentive to the weight of her words.

She learns when to speak and when silence serves better.
She learns how to offer truth without harm.
She learns to encourage without exaggeration.
She learns to correct without contempt.

Wisdom shapes not only what she says, but how and when she says it. Her voice becomes trustworthy—not because it is loud or constant, but because it is grounded in clarity, compassion, and restraint.

In a world that rewards immediacy and opinion, a wise woman becomes a steady presence. Her words carry peace because they come from a settled place.

Wisdom That Sees the Long View

Faith steadies the heart, and wisdom broadens the horizon. With time, a woman begins to recognize that not every situation requires urgency, not every conflict requires engagement, and not every emotion needs immediate expression.

Wisdom teaches her to step back and consider the longer story God is writing. It helps her discern which battles shape growth and which ones only exhaust the soul. It frees her from being ruled by the moment and anchors her in what truly matters.

This perspective brings peace—not because life is simple, but because her footing is secure. Wisdom cultivates patience. It strengthens resilience. It allows her to move through difficult seasons without losing her grounding.

A Woman of Valor learns to see beyond the immediate. She notices God's slow, faithful work unfolding over time, shaping her life with care.

Wisdom as a Lifelong Companion

Wisdom is never finished. It continues to grow through Scripture, prayer, practice, experience, and community. A wise woman remains teachable. She welcomes growth. She learns from mistakes without letting them define her.

She stays open to God's guidance—even when it leads her somewhere unexpected. Wisdom gives her confidence, not in her own certainty, but in God's faithfulness to lead her step by step.

This is *chayil* with clear sight—strength shaped by discernment, steadiness formed through understanding, courage guided by wisdom.

REFLECTIONS

Clarity often arrives quietly. It may come as a settled sense of direction, a gentle shift in perspective, or a new way of seeing a familiar situation. Reflect on moments when God has given you insight recently. These are signs of wisdom forming within you.

Some areas of life call for deeper discernment than others. Consider where things feel complex, layered, or uncertain right now. Wisdom begins by naming those spaces honestly and inviting God into them without rushing the answer.

Your words reveal much about the wisdom you are cultivating. Think back on recent conversations. Notice where your words brought calm or understanding, and where they may have carried tension. Growth often shows up in awareness long before it shows up in change.

Finally, consider the long view. Where might God be inviting you to slow down, to trust timing, or to release control? Wisdom often brings peace not by resolving everything, but by helping you rest in the faithfulness of God as the story continues to unfold.

KINDNESS:

Strength that Moves Towards Others

Kindness is often misunderstood as something gentle and soft. Scripture paints a deeper picture. Kindness—***chesed*** (חֶסֶד) in Hebrew—is covenant loyalty, steadfast love, compassion that acts, mercy that moves toward others with purpose. It is strength turned outward. It is courage expressed through relationship. It is wisdom made visible in how a woman treats people.

The Woman of Valor embodies kindness because her heart has been shaped by God. Her compassion is intentional. Her words carry weight. Her presence brings calm. Kindness is not an accessory to her strength—it is the fruit of it.

Where faith anchors her spirit and wisdom sharpens her discernment, kindness becomes the way she reflects God's character in daily life. It is the texture of her strength.

Kindness as Strength, Not Softness

Kindness requires resilience. It asks you to respond gently when others are sharp. It asks you to listen rather than rush to judgment. It invites forgiveness when resentment would feel easier, and light when criticism would feel justified.

This is not weakness.

This is controlled strength.

Kindness is rooted in the decision to let compassion lead. It is the discipline of seeing others through the eyes of God rather than through the lens of immediate emotion. It requires restraint, patience, and courage—especially when kindness costs something.

The Woman of Valor in Proverbs 31

> *"opens her mouth with wisdom, and the teaching of kindness is on her tongue."*

Her speech carries life because her heart has learned patience, gentleness, and intentional care.

The Power of Words

Words have the power to wound or to heal. Scripture reminds us that the tongue can build up or tear down, bless or break. A Woman of Valor understands this weight. She does not handle language casually.

Her words bring clarity to confusion, comfort to sorrow, and encouragement to those who feel unseen or weary. Her voice becomes a gift—not because it is flawless, but because it is guided by compassion.

She learns to pause before speaking when emotions rise.
She learns to choose honesty without harshness.
She learns to offer correction without contempt.
She learns to encourage others without losing her own grounding.

Kindness gives her voice authority because it gives her words intention.

Kindness That Creates Safety

People are drawn to kindness—not because it avoids truth, but because it offers truth with humility and care. Kindness creates safety. It forms space where others can breathe, speak honestly, and recover strength.

A kind woman becomes a refuge in a world marked by hurry, criticism, and performance. Her presence communicates, *You are seen. You are safe here.*

This form of kindness often appears in quiet ways:
in the way you listen with full attention,
in the grace you extend to someone having a difficult day,
in the patience you offer those closest to you,
in the gentleness you show yourself when discouragement creeps in.

Your kindness quietly reshapes the emotional climate around you. It changes rooms. It changes conversations. It changes lives.

Kindness Toward Oneself

Many women extend compassion to everyone except themselves. Yet the Woman of Valor's kindness must take root inward before it can flow outward. To love others well, she learns to treat her own heart with care.

This means releasing impossible expectations. It means forgiving past mistakes. It means speaking truth to herself without cruelty. It means honoring limits, recognizing needs, and resting without apology.

When you practice kindness toward yourself, you do not grow weaker—you grow steadier. You become more resilient, more patient, and more capable of offering genuine compassion to others.

Self-kindness is not indulgence.
It is emotional stewardship.

Kindness That Reflects God's Heart

God's kindness is not passive. It moves. It restores. It protects. It remains faithful. Throughout Scripture, God's *chesed* carries people through wilderness, failure, and fear.

When you walk in kindness, you reflect this aspect of God's character.

Kindness becomes ministry.
It becomes testimony without words.
It becomes legacy formed in ordinary moments.

Your kindness may never be celebrated publicly, but it will be written deeply into the hearts of those who encounter you. This is the enduring strength of *chayil*—compassion with weight, love that perseveres, and gentleness that transforms.

REFLECTIONS

The way you speak carries more influence than you may realize. Tone, timing, and presence shape the emotional environment around you long before words are fully heard. In recent conversations—especially the ordinary ones—you may notice how kindness has already been at work. A softened response, a pause instead of a reaction, a word that steadied rather than escalated.

These moments matter. They reveal how God is forming your voice into something trustworthy and life-giving.

There are also places where kindness feels harder to offer. Moments when frustration rises quickly, when hurt presses close, when reaction feels justified. In those spaces, kindness becomes an act of courage. It asks you to slow down, to breathe, and to let compassion guide what comes next. This does not mean ignoring truth or avoiding boundaries. It means allowing strength to remain under God's direction rather than emotion's control.

Kindness is also something your own heart needs. Many women extend grace freely to others while holding themselves to impossible standards. In this season, gentleness toward yourself may be one of the most faithful responses God is inviting you into. Rest without guilt. Speak to yourself with honesty and tenderness. Release the pressure to be endlessly capable. These practices do not diminish your strength—they deepen it.

Finally, consider the quiet reach of your kindness. Somewhere in your life, someone is carrying more than they can say. A listening presence, a thoughtful word, or a simple act of care may become a point of light for them. You may never see the full effect, but God does. Kindness offered in faith leaves an imprint far beyond the moment.

This is the strength of *chayil* made visible—love that moves toward others, compassion that carries weight, and a presence that reflects the steady heart of God.

BUILDING A LIFE OF VALOR:

*Rhythms of Strength: Living a
Life of Valor*

Valor grows quietly—in habits repeated over time, in choices made when no one is watching, in the slow and steady shaping of character. While Ruth, Hannah, Deborah, and Sarah show us strength in particular seasons, the Woman of Valor in Proverbs 31 offers something just as powerful: a portrait of everyday faithfulness. Her strength is woven into ordinary life—faith expressed through work, wisdom shaping decisions, kindness guiding relationships.

Modern life rarely slows down on its own. Days are full, attention is fractured, and expectations press in from every side. Family responsibilities, work demands, community needs, financial pressures, emotional labor, and private hopes all compete for space in the heart. In this environment, strength is not only a spiritual calling—it becomes a practical necessity. Without intention, even the strongest woman can find herself depleted.

A life of *chayil* is not built through intensity or constant effort. It is sustained through rhythms—patterns that steady the mind, nourish the heart, and anchor the spirit in God's presence. These rhythms are not rules to master but invitations to live with depth and awareness.

Faith Rooted in Daily Life

Faith grows through consistency far more than through dramatic moments. A Woman of Valor learns to return her heart to God again and again throughout the day. Sometimes this looks like beginning the morning with a simple prayer or a verse that settles the soul before the rush begins. Sometimes it means carrying Scripture with her—listening while driving, reading during a quiet break, or keeping words of truth close at hand. And often, faith is nurtured at day's end, in honest reflection—naming gratitude, acknowledging struggle, and recognizing where God's presence was felt.

These practices do not require hours or perfection. They require intention. Faith is strengthened not by keeping score, but by staying connected.

Wisdom Formed Through Discernment

Wisdom flourishes where there is space to think clearly. It grows in lives that allow for pause—moments where responses are shaped rather than reactive, where decisions are weighed rather than rushed. A woman of wisdom learns to slow her inner pace, creating room for prayer, reflection, and counsel.

Discernment often comes through asking quieter questions: Does this align with God's character? Does it cultivate peace? Does it reflect the person I am becoming? Wisdom also values the voices of others—trusted friends, mentors, and leaders who speak truth with grace. Over time, patterns emerge. Writing, reflecting, and paying attention to one's own inner life can reveal how God is guiding and shaping decisions.

Wisdom is not about having all the answers. It is about making room to see clearly.

Kindness as a Way of Being

Kindness becomes a rhythm when it flows from inner steadiness rather than obligation. It shows up in speech that builds rather than wounds, in presence that listens rather than rushes, in small acts of care that soften difficult moments. Kindness is not accidental—it is chosen.

It is also directed inward. A Woman of Valor extends compassion to herself, releasing perfectionism, honoring limits, and allowing rest without guilt. Kindness grows where there is gentleness, patience, and purposeful care—for others and for one's own heart.

Rest as a Sacred Practice

Rest is not a sign of weakness. It is a requirement for sustained strength. Even the Woman of Valor rests. Her life is not driven by constant motion but shaped by cycles of work and renewal. She learns where to draw boundaries, when to pause, and how to step back without fear.

Sabbath rhythms—however they are practiced—create space for the soul to breathe. Restorative practices such as walking, journaling, quiet music, or time in nature reconnect the heart to God's presence. Sleep, too, is sacred. The body is not an obstacle to spiritual life but a vessel to be cared for.

A life of valor is only sustainable when rest is woven into its foundation.

Service That Flows from Love

The Woman of Valor is generous because generosity flows naturally from a heart shaped by God. She opens her hands to those in need, not from pressure but from overflow. Service becomes a rhythm when it is purposeful and aligned with calling.

Sometimes this looks like blessing a community, mentoring another woman, or offering help where it is needed. Sometimes it means supporting family with patience, encouragement, and emotional presence. And often, it is expressed through the intentional use of one's gifts—leadership, hospitality, creativity, wisdom—offered with love.

She does not do everything. She does what God places before her, faithfully.

Gratitude That Reorients the Heart

Gratitude is a quiet discipline that reshapes perspective. It trains the heart to notice God's goodness in small and ordinary moments. Beginning the day with a simple thank-you, naming small gifts as they appear, or speaking appreciation aloud—all of these practices cultivate resilience and hope.

Gratitude does not deny hardship. It reorients the soul toward God's presence within it. A grateful heart becomes open, steady, and attentive to grace.

Reflection

The rhythms of your days are shaping you, often more than you realize. Some patterns strengthen your inner life, bringing peace, clarity, and a sense of God's nearness. Others slowly drain you, leaving fatigue where joy once lived. Paying attention to these rhythms is an act of wisdom, not self-focus. It is how strength becomes sustainable.

Valor is rarely formed through sweeping changes. It grows through small, faithful practices—moments of prayer, quiet reflection, gentle words chosen with care. These seemingly ordinary choices accumulate over time, forming a resilience that holds steady when life presses hard.

There are also places where rest may be calling louder than effort. Weariness often carries wisdom. When exhaustion begins to overshadow joy, it may be an invitation from God to reorder priorities, release unnecessary weight, or allow rest to become part of faithfulness. Strength deepens when striving gives way to trust.

And even now, more valor is present in your life than you may see. In responsibilities carried with care. In kindness offered without recognition. In perseverance that keeps showing up on ordinary days. These are not small things. They are the quiet evidence of *chayil* already taking root—strength being formed patiently, faithfully, and deeply within you.

This is how a Woman of Valor lives. Not by striving to become someone else, but by allowing God to shape strength through the steady rhythms of an ordinary, faithful life.

BECOMING AN ESHET CHAYIL IN TODAYS WORLD:

The Woman of Valor does not belong only to the ancient world. Her strength has never been bound to time, geography, or culture. The courage, wisdom, and faith celebrated in Proverbs 31 are not relics of a distant age—they are deeply needed now, in a world marked by speed, pressure, confusion, and shifting expectations.

The modern woman navigates a landscape very different from Ruth's fields or Deborah's courtroom beneath the palm tree. Her challenges may involve deadlines instead of harvests, digital overload instead of tribal conflict, and emotional labor instead of nomadic travel. But the weight is real, and the need for strength is no less pressing.

Becoming an *Eshet Chayil* today does not mean reproducing the tasks of the ancient poem. Rather it should embody the same depth of character, the same steadiness of spirit, and the same faith-rooted courage within the complexities of contemporary life.

Valor is timeless. It simply takes new forms.

Courage in a Culture of Noise

Modern life is loud. News cycles churn, opinions multiply, notifications demand attention, and comparison creeps in through glowing screens. In this environment, courage often looks quieter than we expect. It appears in the deliberate creation of silence, in the decision to step away from constant input long enough to listen for God's voice.

A modern Woman of Valor learns to guard her inner life. She chooses presence in a world addicted to distraction. She honors stillness in a culture that equates worth with productivity. She understands that clarity is cultivated, not stumbled upon.

In a digital age, valor often begins with the courage to disconnect—not out of fear, but out of wisdom. Silence becomes a form of resistance. Attention becomes an act of faith.

Wisdom in a World of Confusion

Never before has so much information been so readily available—and never before has discernment been so necessary. Opinions often masquerade as truth, emotional reactions are rewarded over thoughtful reflection, and speed is valued more than depth.

Wisdom for the modern woman includes the ability to slow down. To evaluate what she hears through the lens of Scripture. To seek truth rather than approval. To resist the pull of trends and remain anchored when cultural winds shift.

A Woman of Valor does not rush to conclusions. She listens carefully. She weighs her responses. She understands that clarity often comes through patience. Where others react quickly, she responds wisely. Where others chase influence, she pursues integrity.

In a world hungry for certainty, wisdom becomes a stabilizing presence.

Kindness in a Wounded World

Despite unprecedented connection, the modern world carries deep fracture. Voices are amplified, but so are criticism, comparison, and isolation. In such a climate, kindness becomes a powerful force.

A modern Woman of Valor understands the weight her words carry—spoken, written, and implied. She chooses language that heals rather than harms. She practices empathy in a culture quick to judge. She remembers that gentleness is not weakness and compassion is not passivity.

Kindness becomes her countercultural strength. Through it, she creates pockets of peace. She becomes a steady presence where others feel unseen or overwhelmed. She does not merely exist within the world as it is—she quietly reshapes it.

Strength in a World That Expects Too Much

Women today are often expected to excel in every sphere simultaneously—career, family, relationships, health, appearance, spirituality, and social awareness—always with grace and composure. These expectations create a pressure Proverbs 31 was never meant to impose.

Modern strength often looks like restraint. It may mean saying no without guilt, asking for help without shame, acknowledging limits, and releasing perfectionism. It involves allowing God—not culture—to define success.

A Woman of Valor understands that she is not meant to be everything to everyone. She is called to faithfulness, not exhaustion. Boundaries become acts of wisdom. Rest becomes an expression of trust. Discernment shapes how she gives her energy.

Valor today includes knowing what to release.

Faithfulness Beyond Achievement

Proverbs 31 honors diligence, but not frantic striving. It celebrates fruitfulness rooted in purpose, not performance. In a world obsessed with visibility and achievement, faithfulness becomes a radical choice.

A modern Woman of Valor lives with consistency rather than chaos. She honors commitments without losing herself. She nurtures relationships with presence. She pursues excellence without idolizing success. Her integrity holds firm even when no one is watching.

Her worth is anchored in God, not applause. Her identity rests in who she is becoming, not in what she produces.

Strength That Grows in Community

No woman becomes *Eshet Chayil* alone. Ruth had Naomi. Hannah had Eli. Deborah had Barak. Sarah had Abraham. Strength in Scripture is always communal.

For the modern woman, community may take many forms— mentors who speak truth, friends who share burdens, spiritual companions who pray, younger women who learn by watching, family members who shape daily life. Valor grows when women walk together.

Community creates space for both giving and receiving strength. It allows wisdom to become generational. It transforms individual courage into shared resilience.

Becoming an *Eshet Chayil* today means choosing connection over isolation and allowing strength to be formed not only within you, but among you.

Reflection

You may already be living as a Woman of Valor in ways that feel ordinary or unnoticed. In your workplace, your home, your friendships, and your quiet faithfulness, strength is already taking shape. Wisdom offered gently, peace cultivated in tense spaces, courage practiced in small decisions—these are signs of *chayil* at work.

At the same time, modern pressures can weigh heavily. Overcommitment, constant connectivity, comparison, and unspoken expectations can drain the spirit. These burdens often reveal where God is inviting you to release what was never meant to be carried and to rest more deeply in His grace.

Courage in today's world is rarely dramatic. It shows up in boundaries set with clarity, truth spoken with kindness, pace slowed intentionally, and faith practiced steadily. Valor grows through daily choices that align your life with God's wisdom.

And strength deepens in community. The relationships that nurture you—and the ones where you offer presence and care—are part of how God forms courage over time. You were never meant to walk this path alone.

This is what it means to become an *Eshet Chayil* today. Not by striving to meet impossible standards, but by living faithfully, wisely, and courageously in the world God has placed you in.

A LEGACY OF VALOR:

The Woman Who Impacts Generations

Legacy is the imprint you leave long after your words have faded, your tasks are finished, and your seasons have passed. It is carried forward in the lives you touched, the wisdom you offered, the faith you modeled, and the strength you bore with humility. Long after a woman passes from one chapter of life to another, her presence continues to echo through the people who were shaped by her.

A Woman of Valor does not set out to create a legacy. She sets out to live faithfully. Legacy is simply the quiet harvest of that faithfulness.

Scripture makes this clear through the lives we have already encountered. Ruth's loyalty becomes part of a royal lineage. Hannah's prayers shape a prophet. Deborah's leadership steadies a nation. Sarah's faith becomes foundational to Israel itself. None of these women began with the goal of becoming remembered. They began with choices—ordinary, courageous, faithful choices. Over time, those choices shaped futures far beyond what they could see.

Legacy is formed the same way today.

Legacy Rooted in Identity

Legacy flows from who you are, not from what you accumulate. Strength, faith, wisdom, and kindness leave marks that outlast accomplishments, titles, and roles. When a woman knows who she is in God, her presence becomes formative. Her steadiness offers refuge. Her wisdom becomes a guiding voice. Her faith becomes something others lean on when their own feels fragile. Her courage becomes an inheritance.

People learn not only from what you say, but from how you live. Children, friends, communities, and younger women absorb the quiet consistency of character over time. Long before legacy becomes visible in the world, it begins taking shape in the heart.

Legacy Grown Through Relationship

A Woman of Valor leaves her deepest imprint through the relationships she nurtures. She invests in people with patience and presence, choosing connection over efficiency and attentiveness over urgency. She notices those who feel overlooked, listens to those who are hurting, and supports those who are still finding their footing.

Relationships become the soil where influence grows. Through prayer, encouragement, forgiveness, and example, her life begins to shape others in ways that feel both natural and enduring. A legacy built through relationship lasts because it is written on hearts rather than on platforms.

Legacy Formed Through Faithfulness Over Time

Valor is not loud or rushed. It is steady, persistent, and patient. Legacy is rarely the result of a single defining moment. More often, it is woven slowly through decades of showing up—especially when it is difficult or unnoticed.

Faithfulness is choosing integrity when no one is watching, keeping promises when it would be easier not to, speaking truth with care, and remaining steady even when life takes an unexpected turn. The world celebrates sudden success, but Scripture honors the long walk of obedience. A Woman of Valor understands that her influence grows the way roots do—quietly deepening with each faithful choice.

Legacy Shaped by Spiritual Maturity

Spiritual maturity reveals itself over time. It shows up in trust that has been tested, in gentleness that has been learned, and in decisions that increasingly reflect God's character. As maturity deepens, a woman's presence begins to steady others. People turn to her not because she has all the answers, but because her life carries perspective.

Younger women seek her wisdom. Friends lean on her discernment. Family members draw stability from her calm. Communities benefit from her grounded faith. This is the quiet authority of a Woman of Valor—authority rooted not in position, but in depth.

Her life becomes a living testimony, preached not from a stage, but through faithfulness.

Legacy That Reaches Beyond a Lifetime

The most meaningful legacies extend beyond a single lifetime. They ripple forward, shaping people a woman may never meet. Through stories told, prayers prayed, traditions formed, and kindness practiced, strength multiplies.

Homes shaped by peace leave traces. Faith passed down becomes courage for another generation. Integrity modeled becomes a path someone else knows how to walk. In this way, a Woman of Valor participates in a story far larger than her own.

Strength lived faithfully becomes strength multiplied.

Legacy as an Invitation

Legacy is not only what you leave behind—it is what you invite others into. A Woman of Valor becomes a doorway rather than a monument. She opens space for others to grow, protects those who are vulnerable, encourages voices still forming, and blesses those who will carry the story forward.

Her life whispers an invitation: *Live with courage. Walk with God. Stay faithful. You can do this too.*

This is the legacy of a Woman of Valor—not perfection, but presence; not control, but faith; not visibility, but depth.

Reflection

Your life is already shaping others, often in ways you cannot see. The steadiness you carry, the compassion you practice, the resilience you embody, and the faith you live out are quietly becoming seeds in the lives around you. These inner qualities are what endure. Long after seasons shift, they remain.

You are also part of a lineage of strength. Women who walked before you—mothers, grandmothers, mentors, teachers, and spiritual guides—left their mark through quiet faithfulness. Their legacy lives on in you, shaping how you love, trust, and persevere. In turn, God invites you to continue that lineage, passing forward what you have received.

Much of what forms legacy happens unseen. Prayers whispered, encouragement offered, patience practiced, forgiveness extended— these small acts carry weight far beyond the moment. God weaves them into a story larger than any one life.

Legacy is not built through pressure or performance. It grows through intention. As you live faithfully, God shapes the imprint your life will leave. And that imprint—formed through courage, wisdom, kindness, and trust—will speak long after the seasons you know have passed.

EPILOGUE

A Blessing for Every Season:

There is a quiet holiness in the journey you have taken through these pages. You have walked with Ruth through the uncertainties of early life. You have prayed with Hannah through longing. You have stood beside Deborah under the shade of her palm tree as she listened, discerned, and led. You have laughed with Sarah—first in disbelief, then in joy—discovering that God's promises reach far beyond the boundaries of time.

Their stories have woven themselves into your own.
Their strength has spoken into your strength.
Their courage has stirred something inside you—something ancient and new all at once.

You have seen that *Eshet Chayil* is not a title earned through perfection. It is a truth awakened through trust. It is a strength that grows in every season: young adulthood, motherhood, leadership, legacy. It is the character God forms, the wisdom He cultivates, the kindness He whispers into your spirit each day.

Your life—every chapter, every hope, every ache, every joy—is held by the same God who shaped theirs. You carry His image. You reflect His strength. You are part of His story. And the strength He forms in you will ripple into the lives of others, long after today's moments become tomorrow's memories.

As you finish this journey, receive this blessing:

A Blessing for the Woman of Valor

May you walk in courage,
even when the way is uncertain,
knowing that God steadies every step.

May wisdom guide your thoughts,
clarifying what matters
and give you clarity in every season.

May kindness shape your words,
making your voice a refuge,
a balm, a source of life for others.

May your faith deepen
through the rhythms of ordinary days—
anchoring you when life is heavy,
lifting you when hope feels distant,
and bringing you peace that cannot be shaken.

May you rest in God's timing,
trusting the slow work He is doing within you,
and may joy rise in unexpected places
as He redeems and restores your story.

May your presence bless your home,
your friendships, your community,
your workplace, and every heart you touch.

May the legacy you leave behind
be one of strength,
of gentleness,
of courage,
of faith,
and of unwavering trust in God.

And may you know—deeply, truly, tenderly—
that you are an **Eshet Chayil**,
a Woman of Valor,

created and cherished by the God
who calls you His own
in every season of your life.

ABOUT THE AUTHOR

Elizabeth Shulam is a Messianic teacher and writer deeply committed to uncovering the Jewish roots of the New Testament and making them accessible for today's reader. She blends careful biblical scholarship, cultural insight, and practical application to guide believers into a richer understanding of God's story and their place within it.

Elizabeth's work includes the "Shalom Y'all" series—which marries academic depth with conversational warmth—and she also joins her husband Barry in "The Blended Kitchen," a creative expression of their shared life, faith, and heritage.

She holds to the conviction that faith is strongest when it is rooted in heritage, lived in community, and applied in everyday life.You can find her on www.jennibet.com or socials:@jennibet_com.